A Collection of Mandalas

Book Three

By

Kim Jordan Blair

I would like to thank my dear friend Renee Kritzer for allowing me to use her colored version of my Umbrella Mandala on the cover of this book.

I would also like to thank Patricia Lavonne Graham Vogelsong for allowing me to use her colored version of the other mandala on the cover of this book.

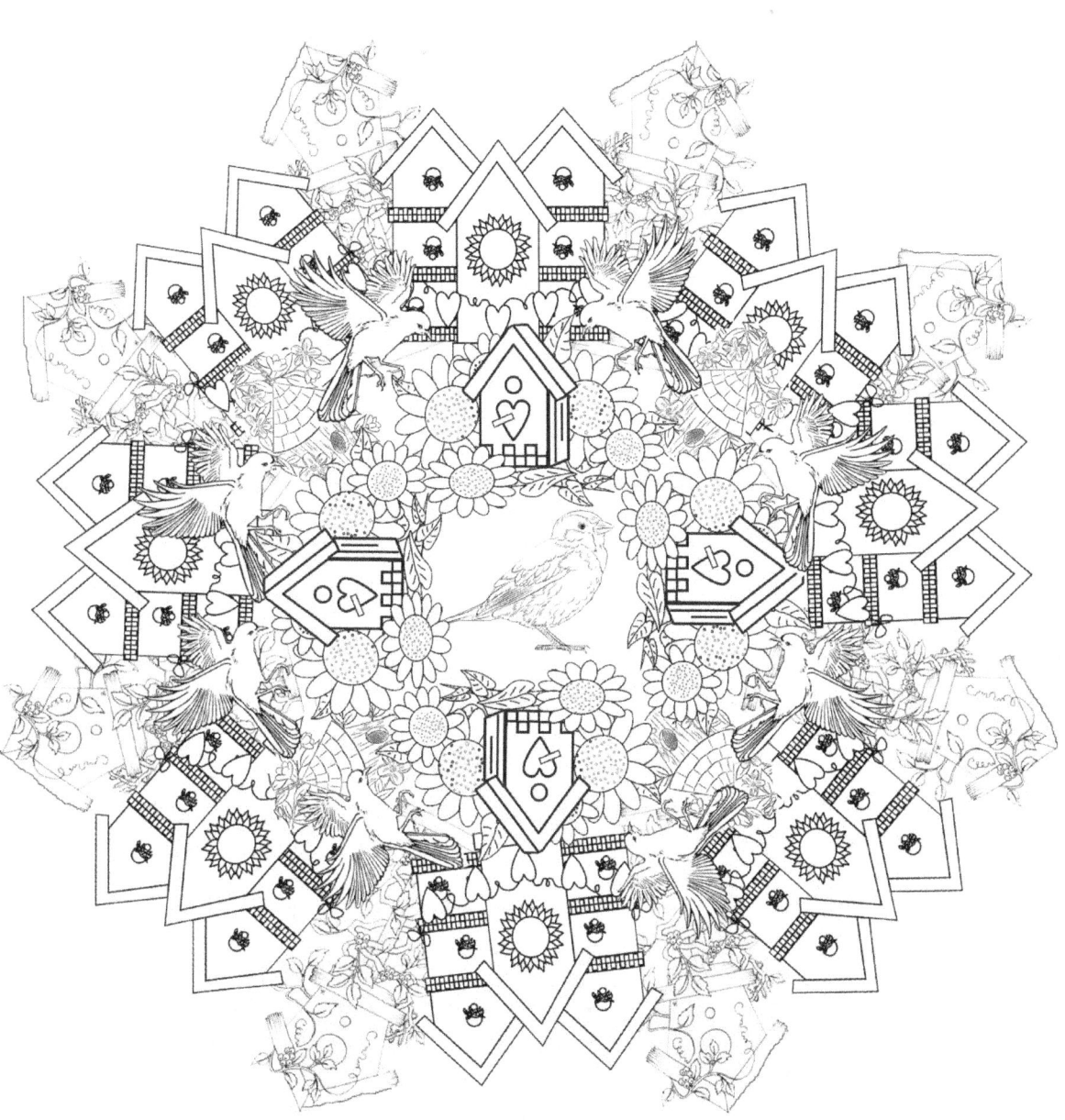

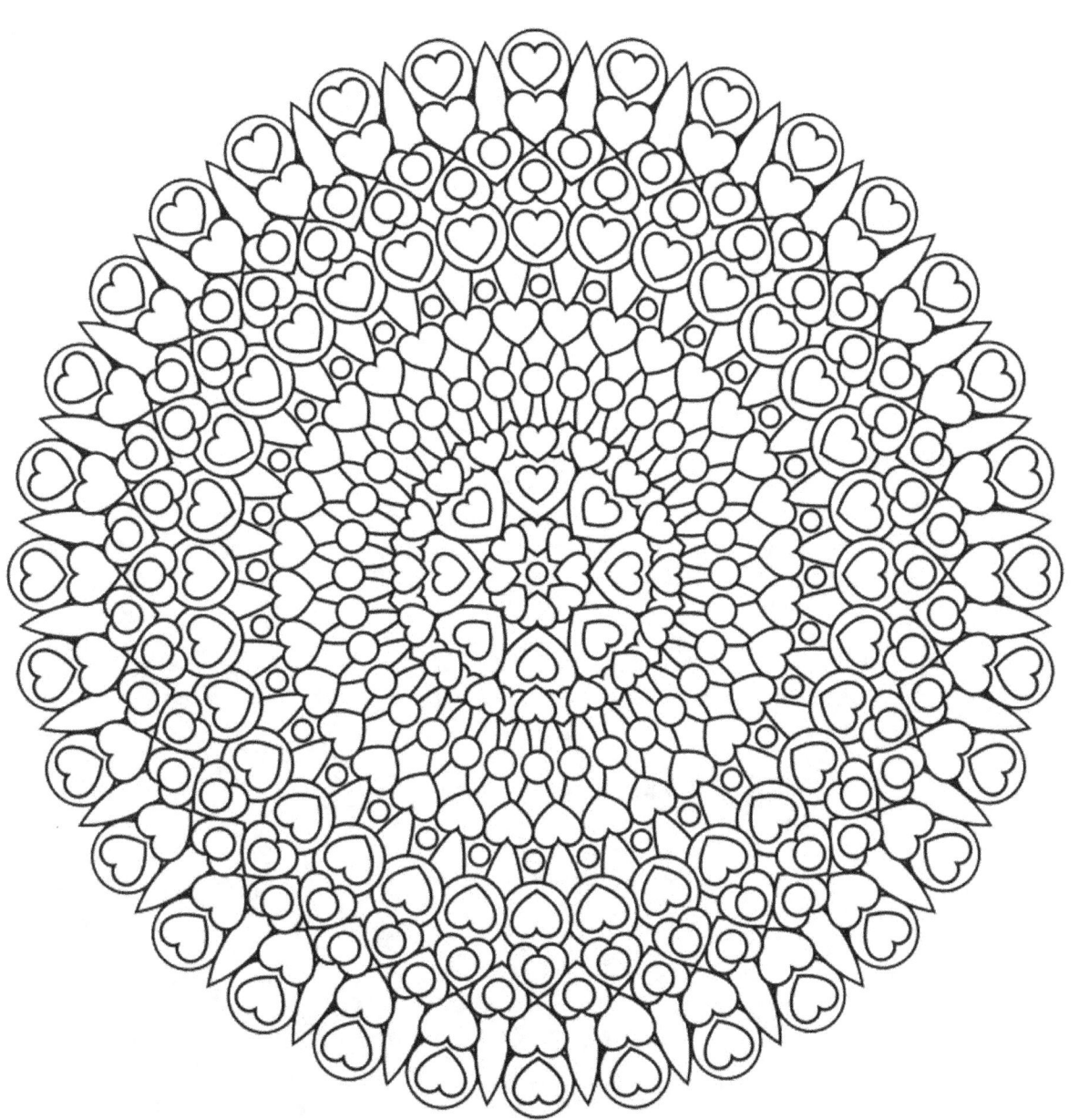

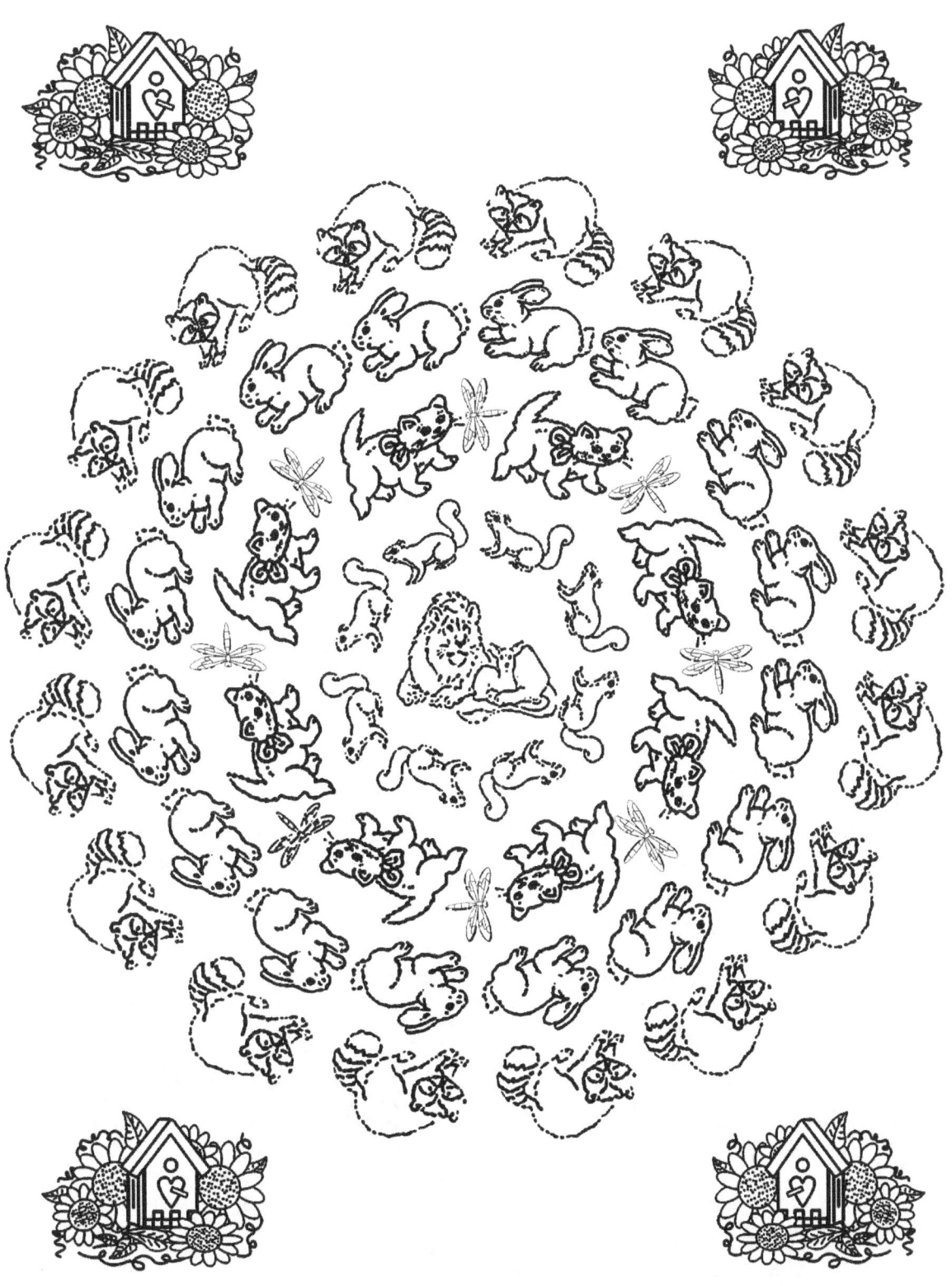

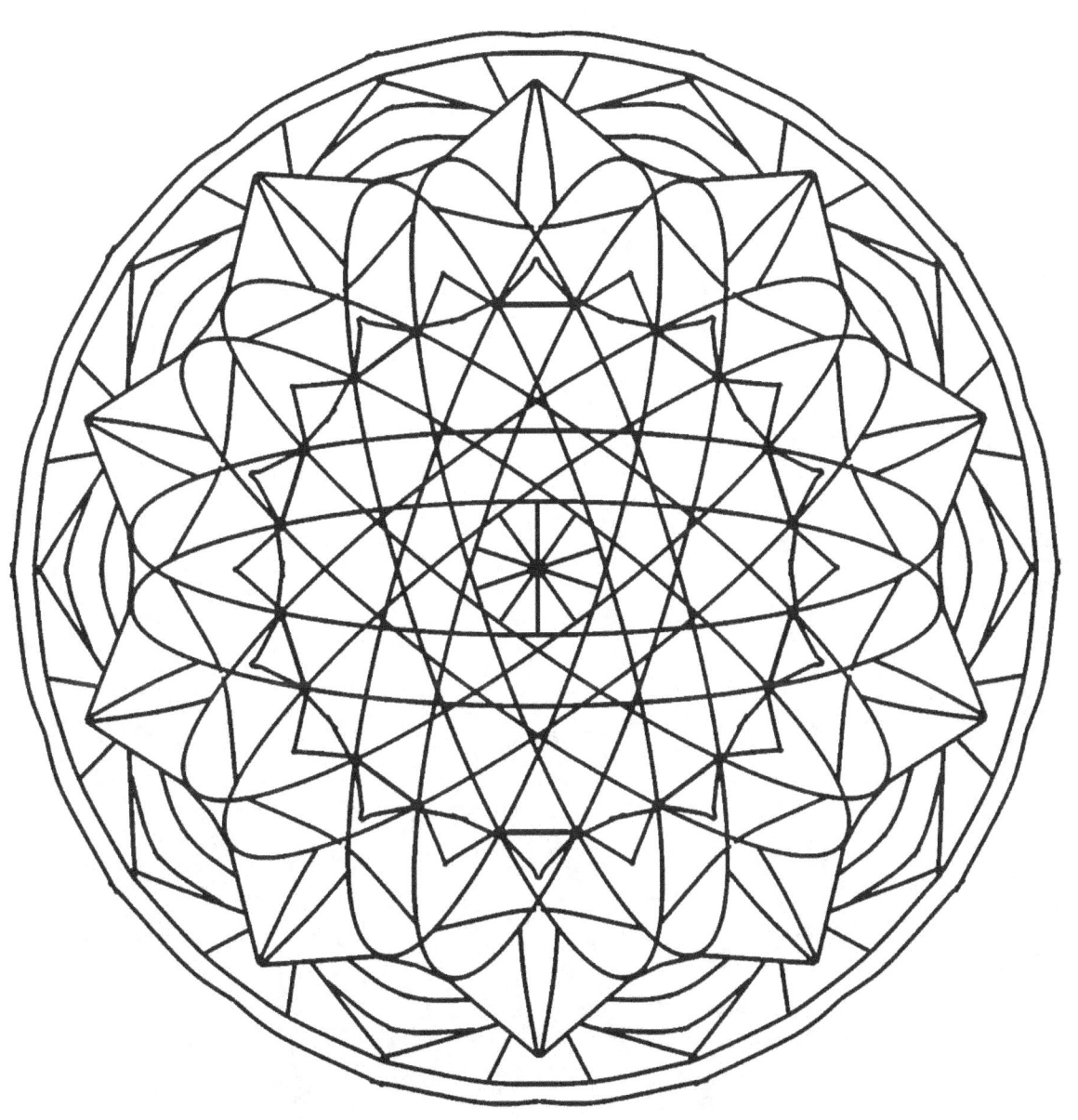

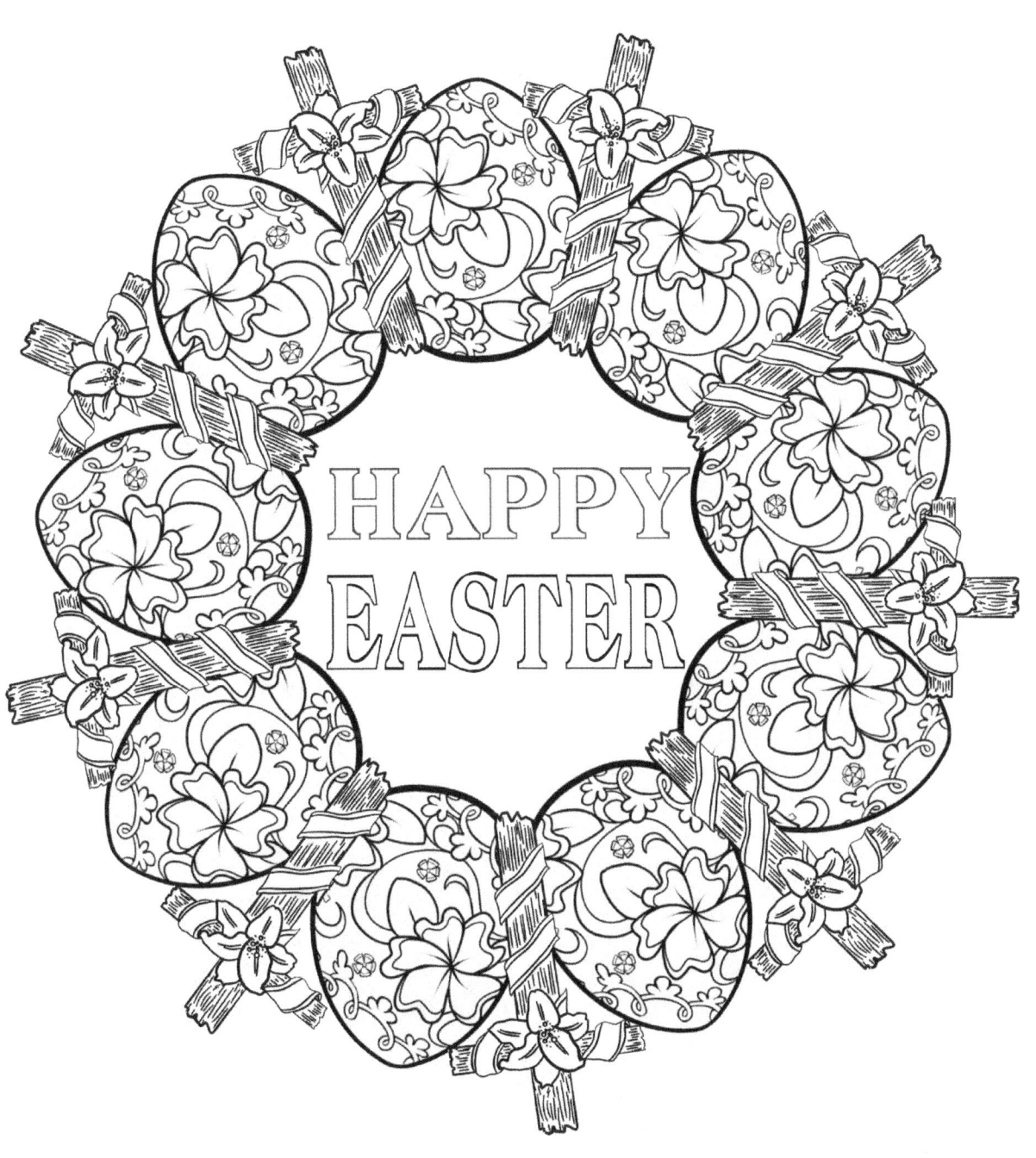

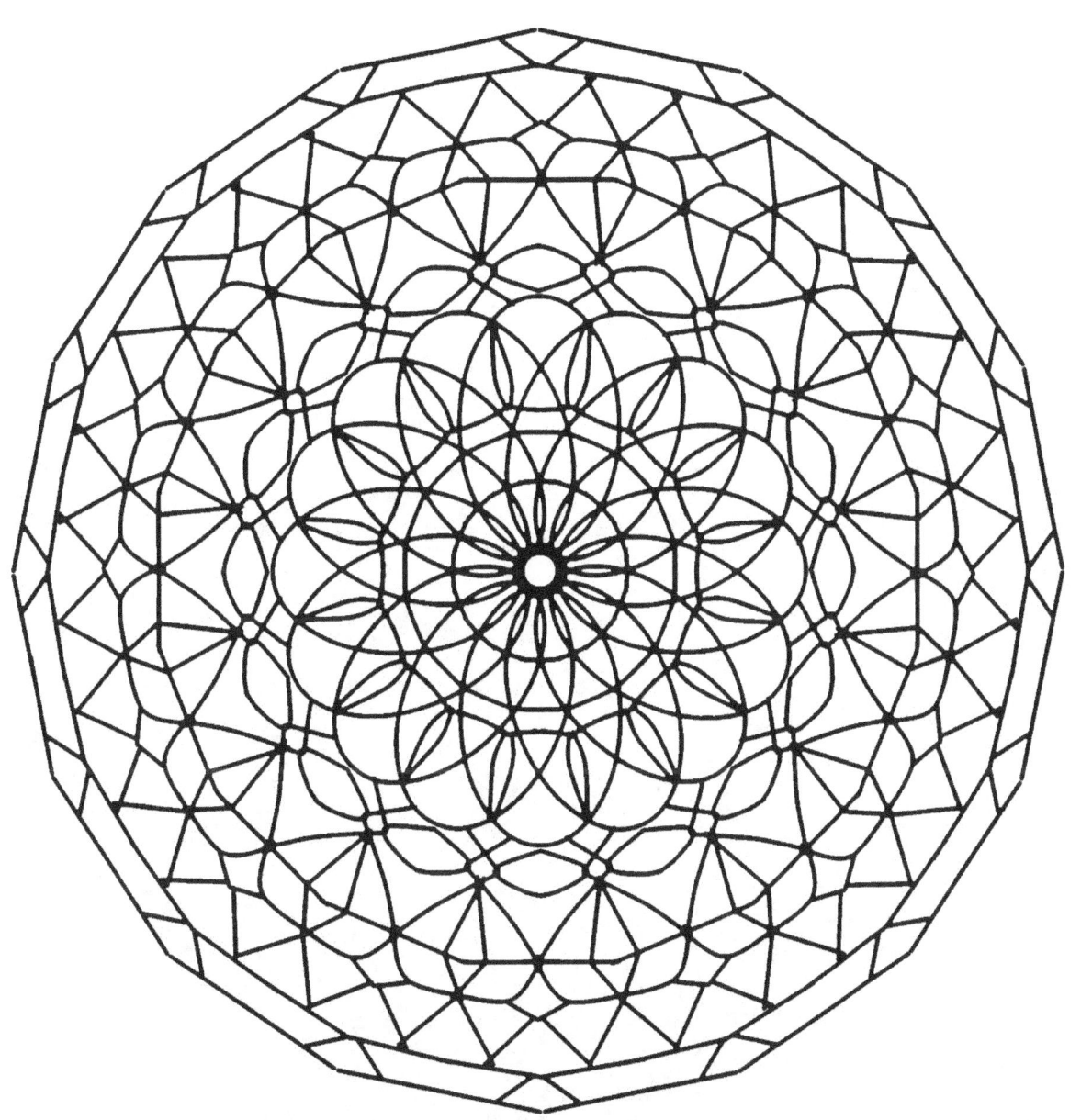

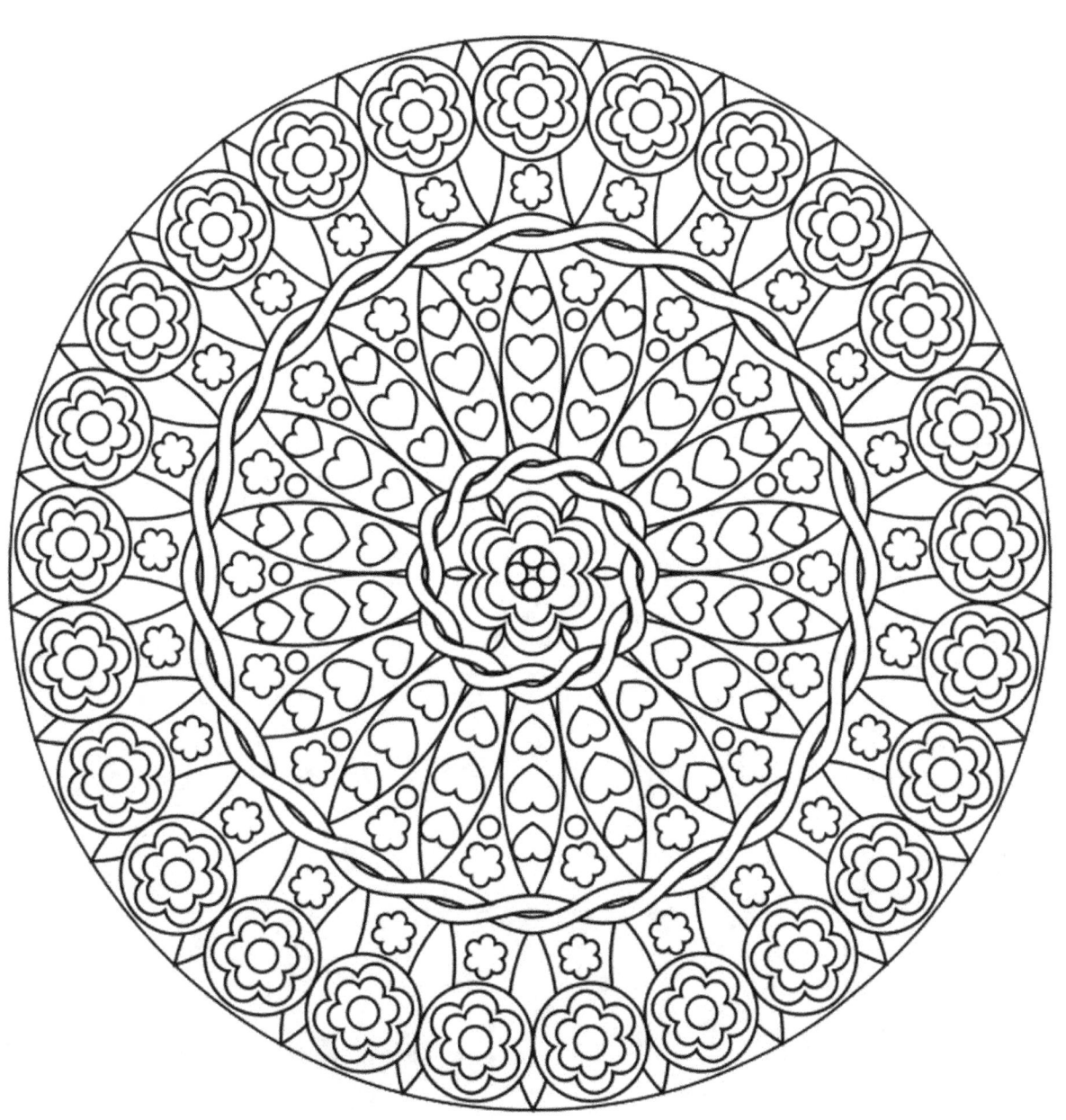

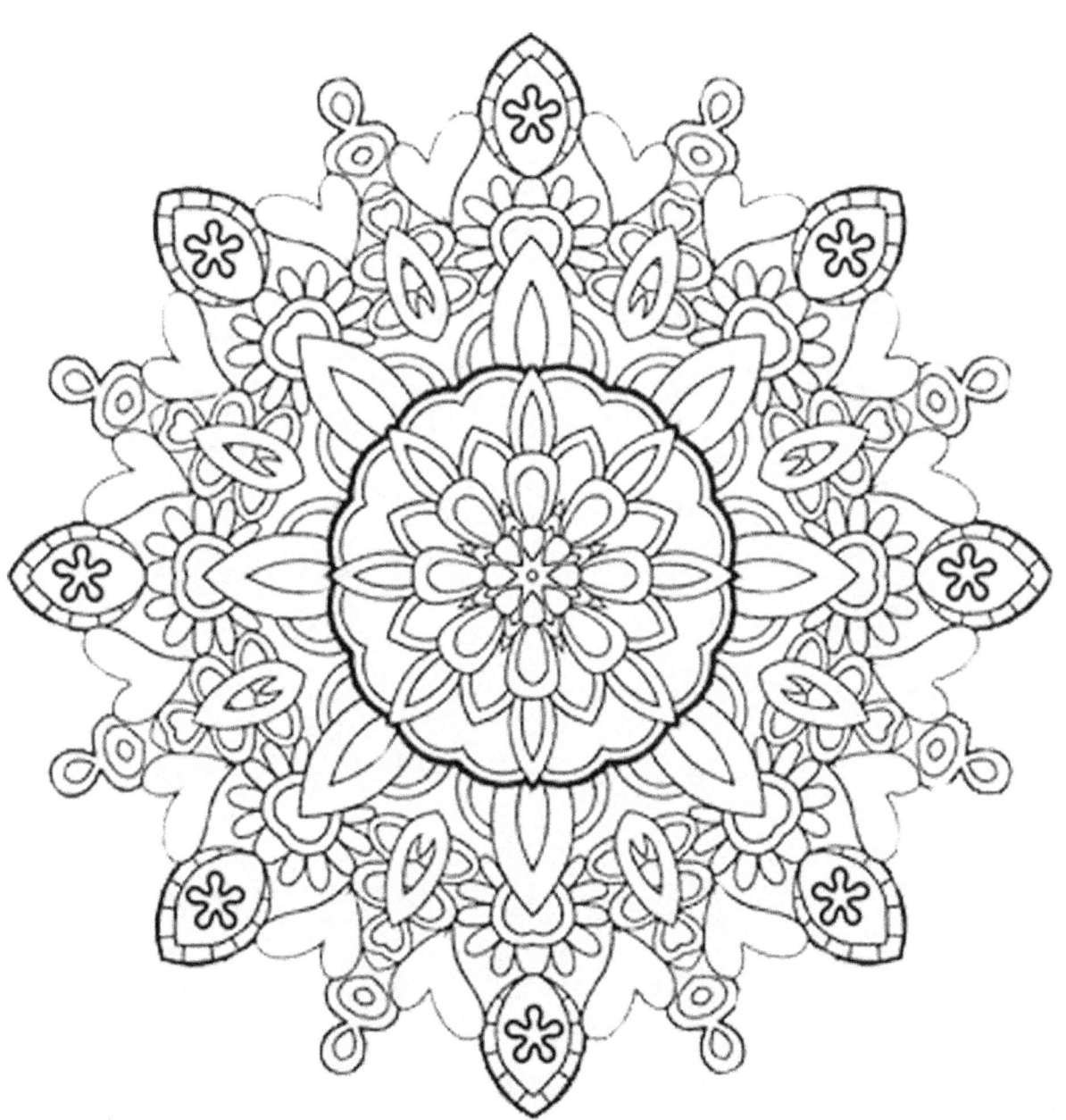

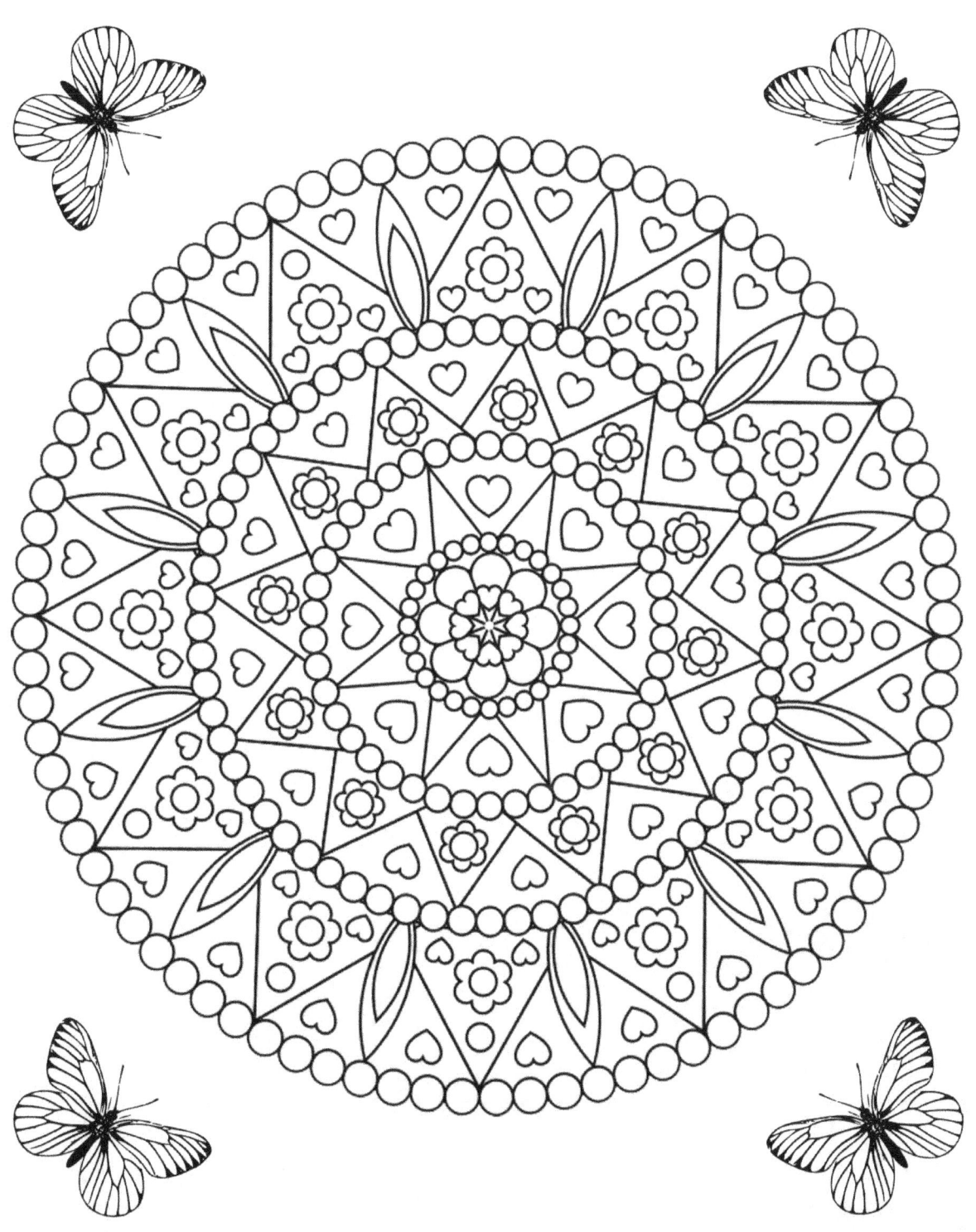

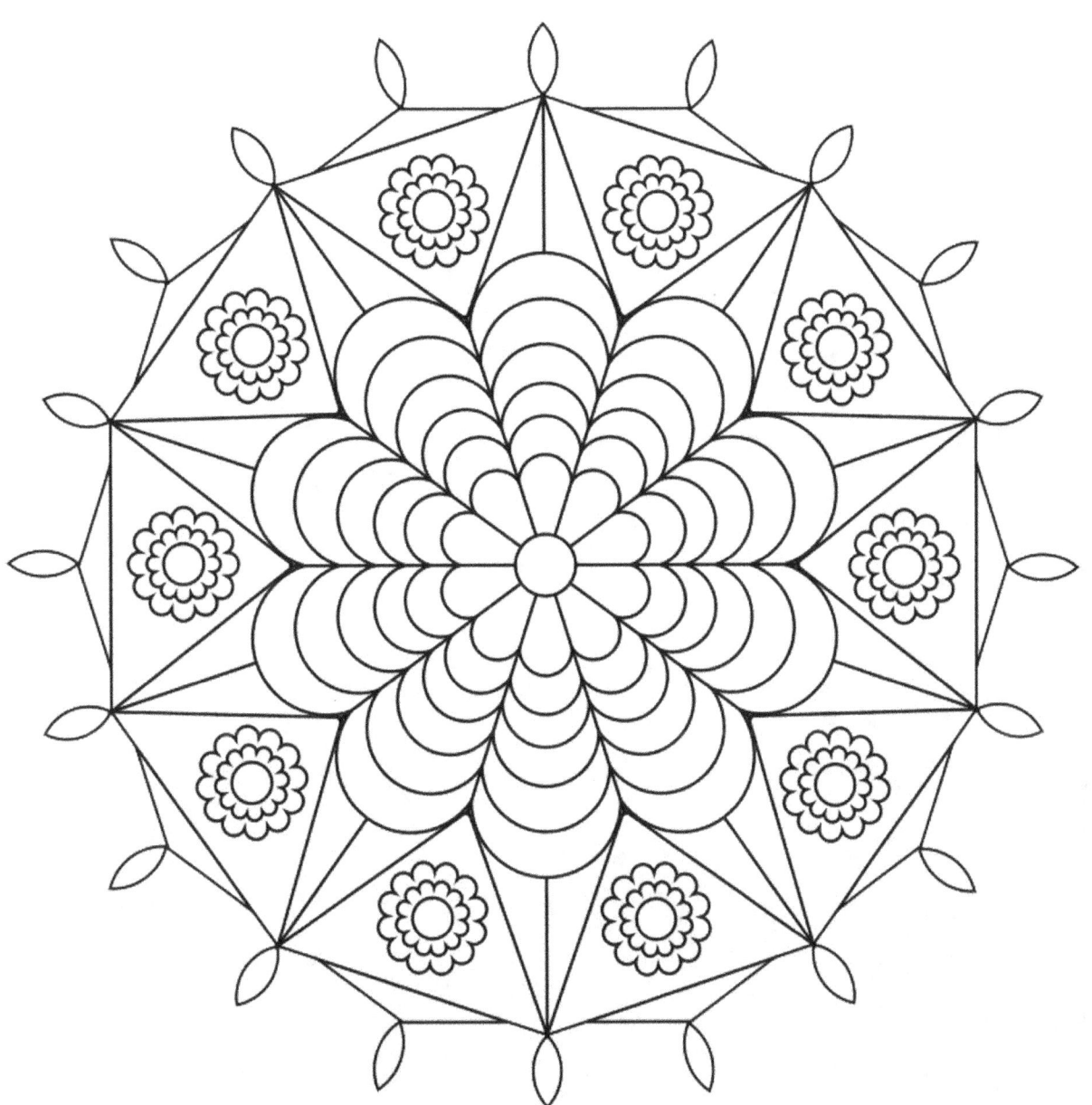

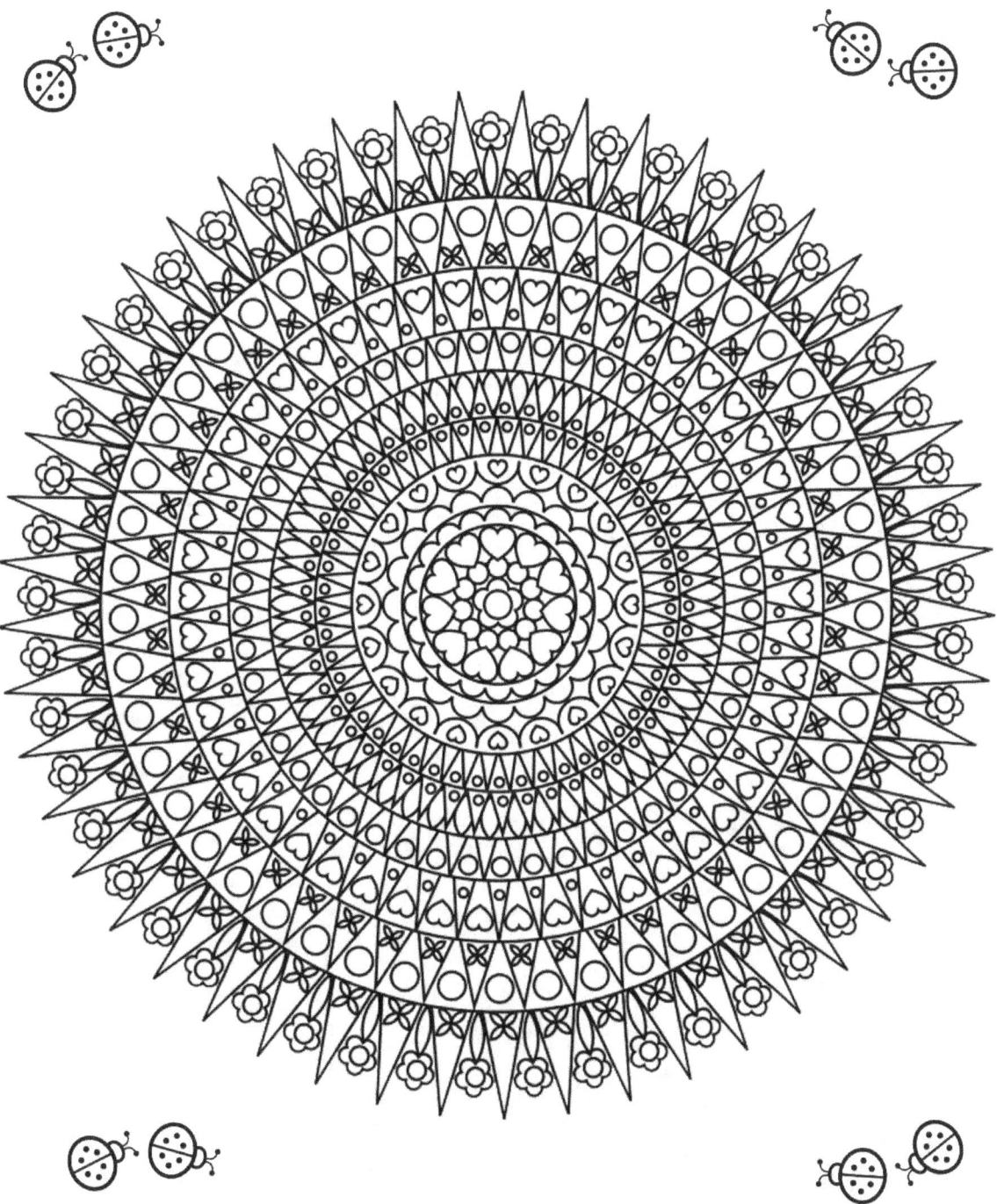

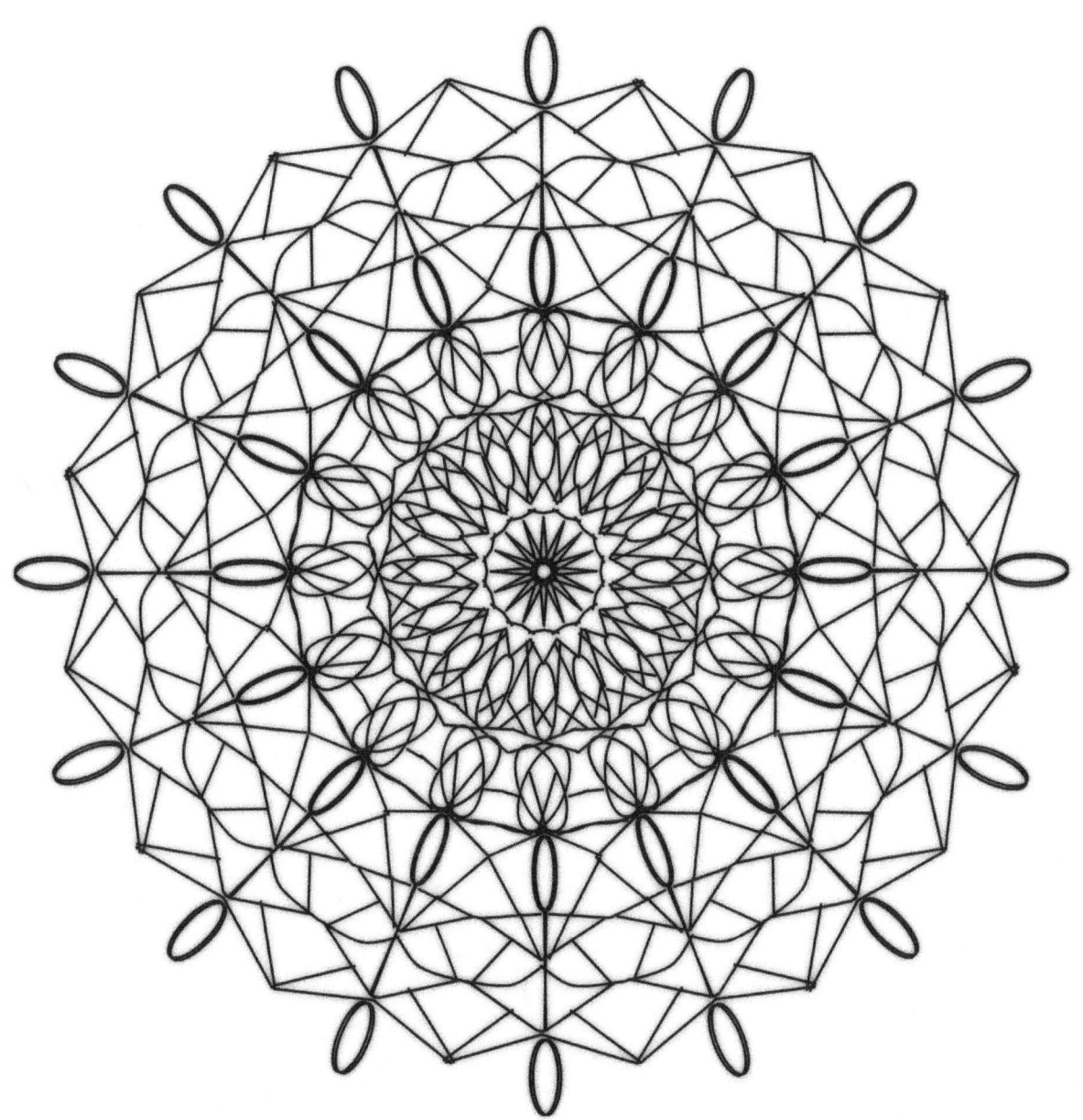

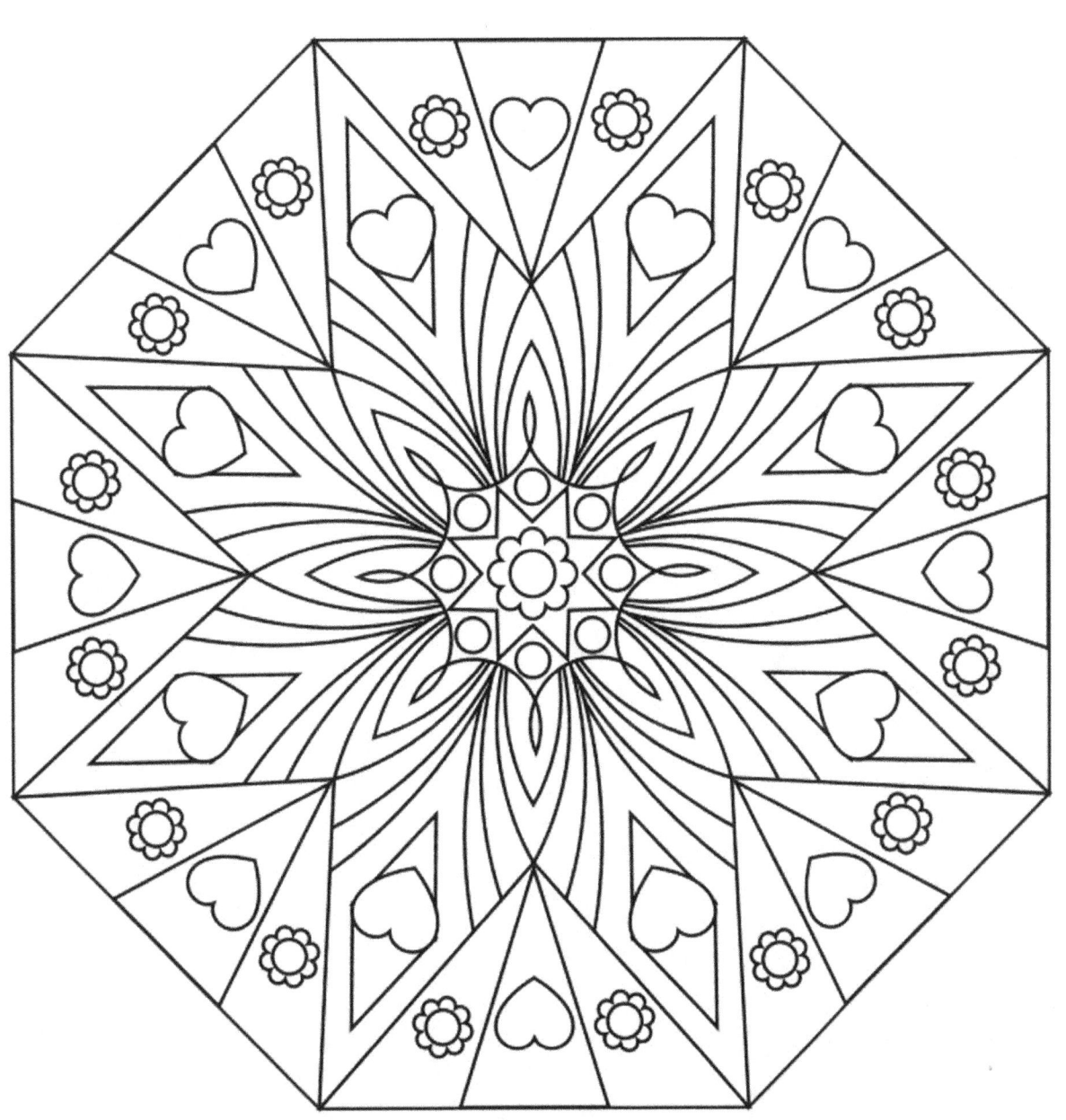

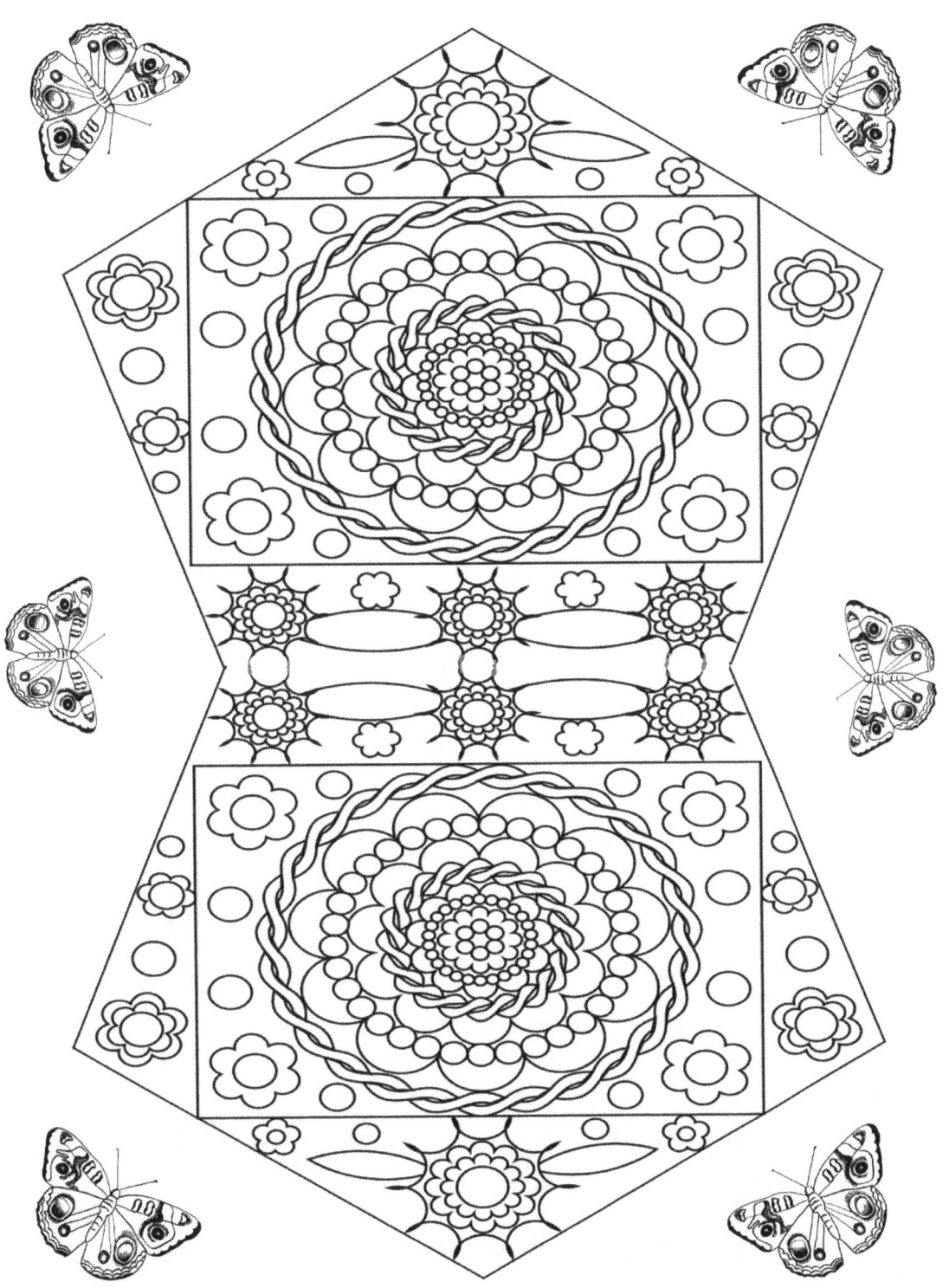

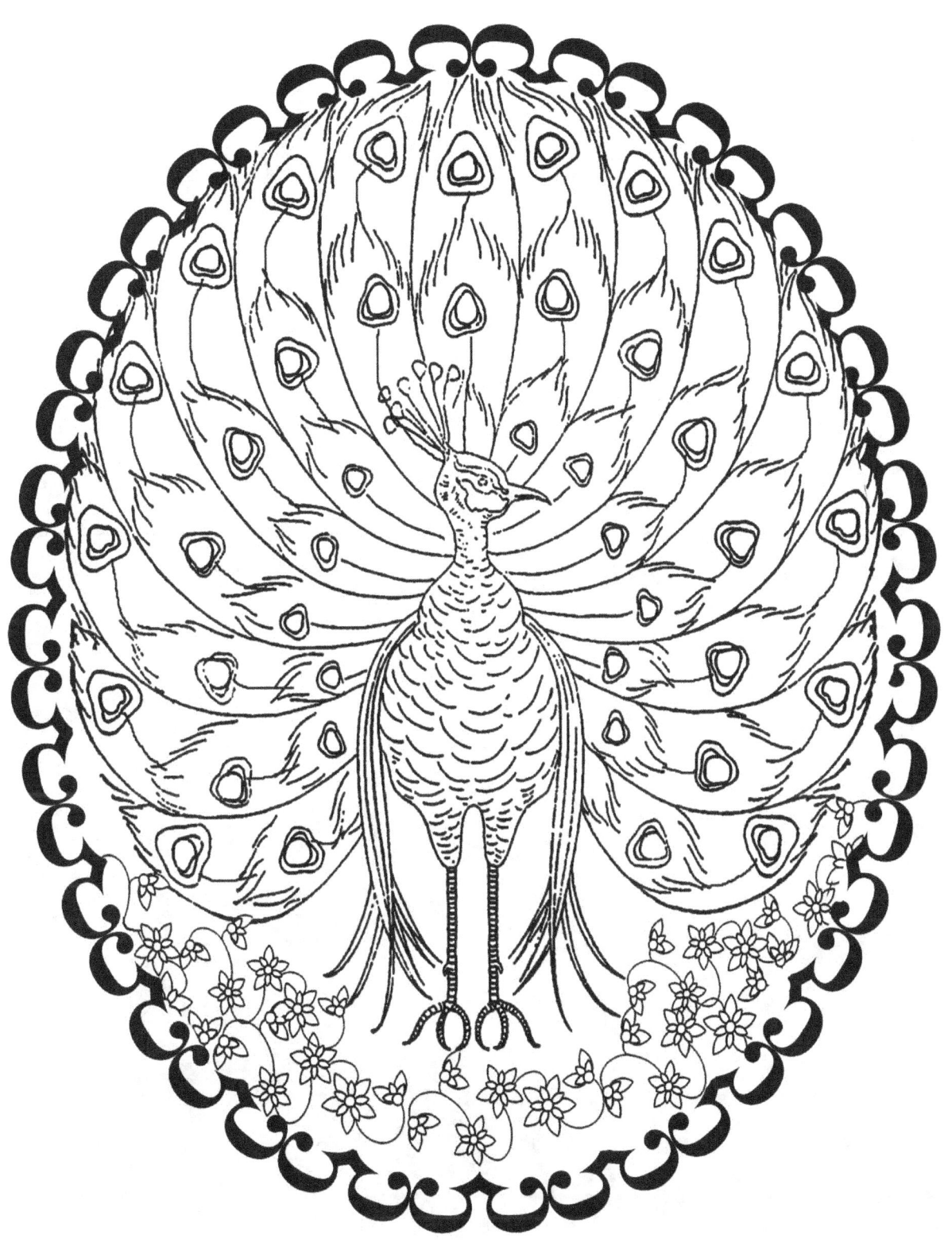

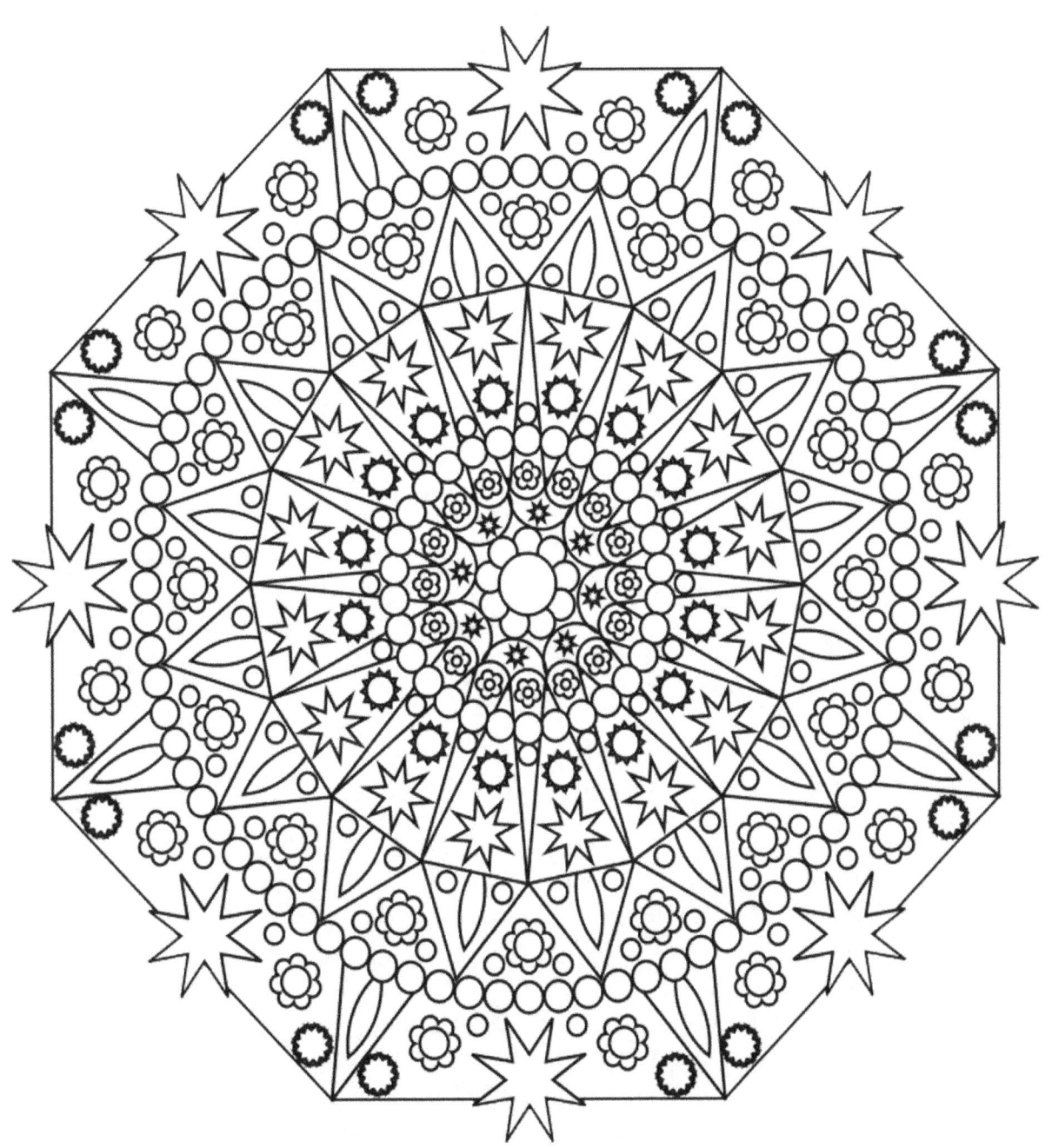

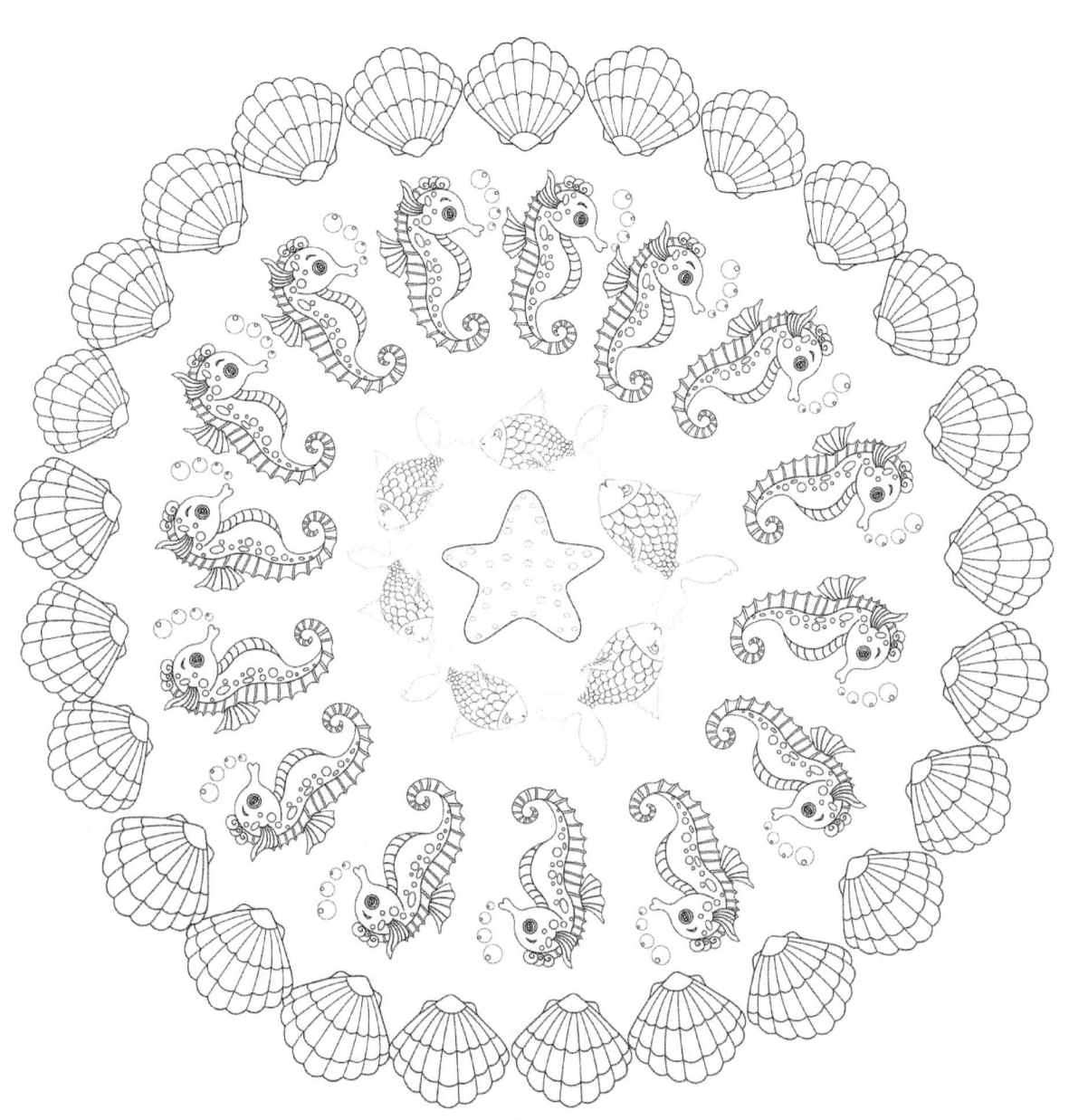

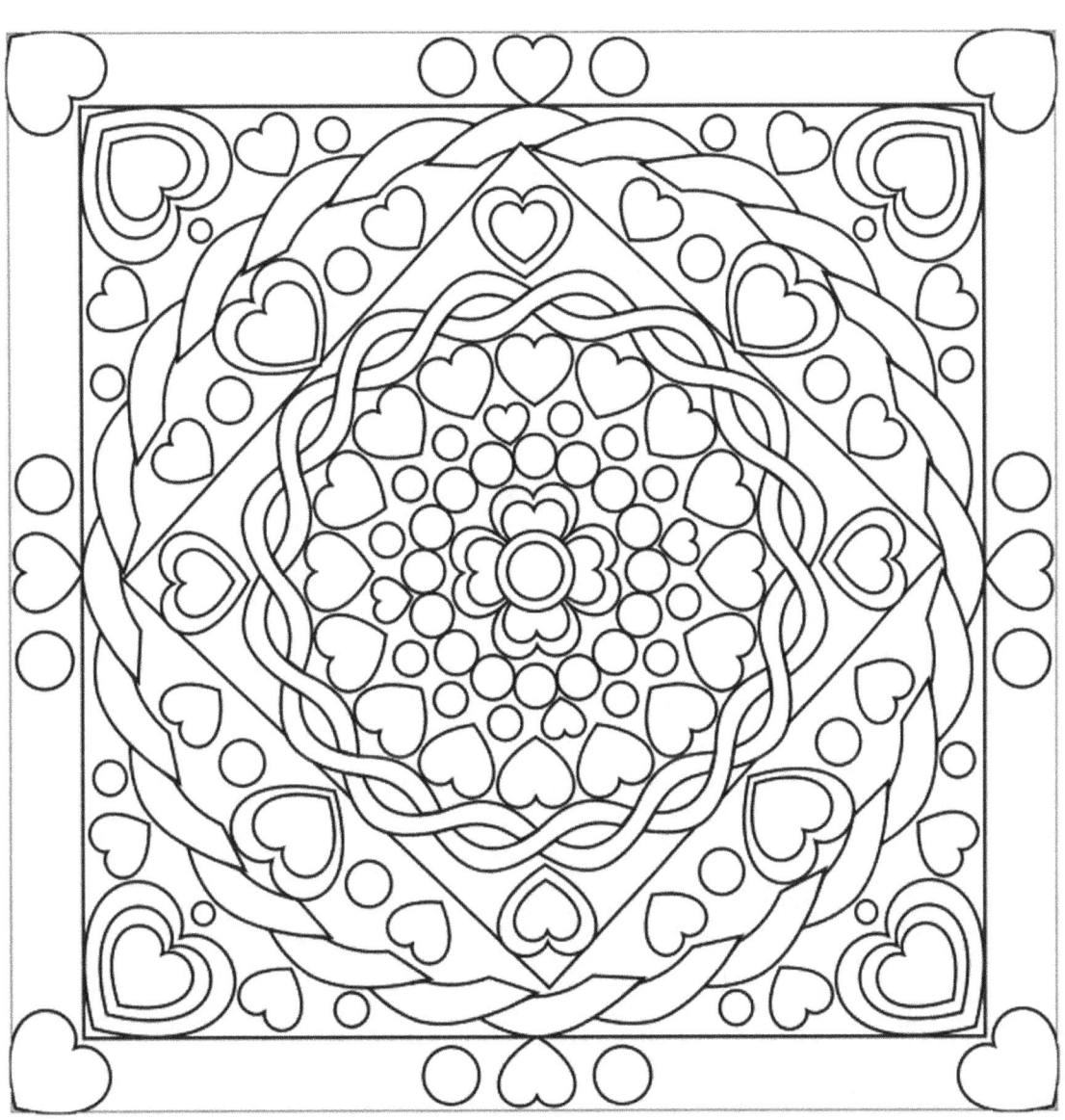

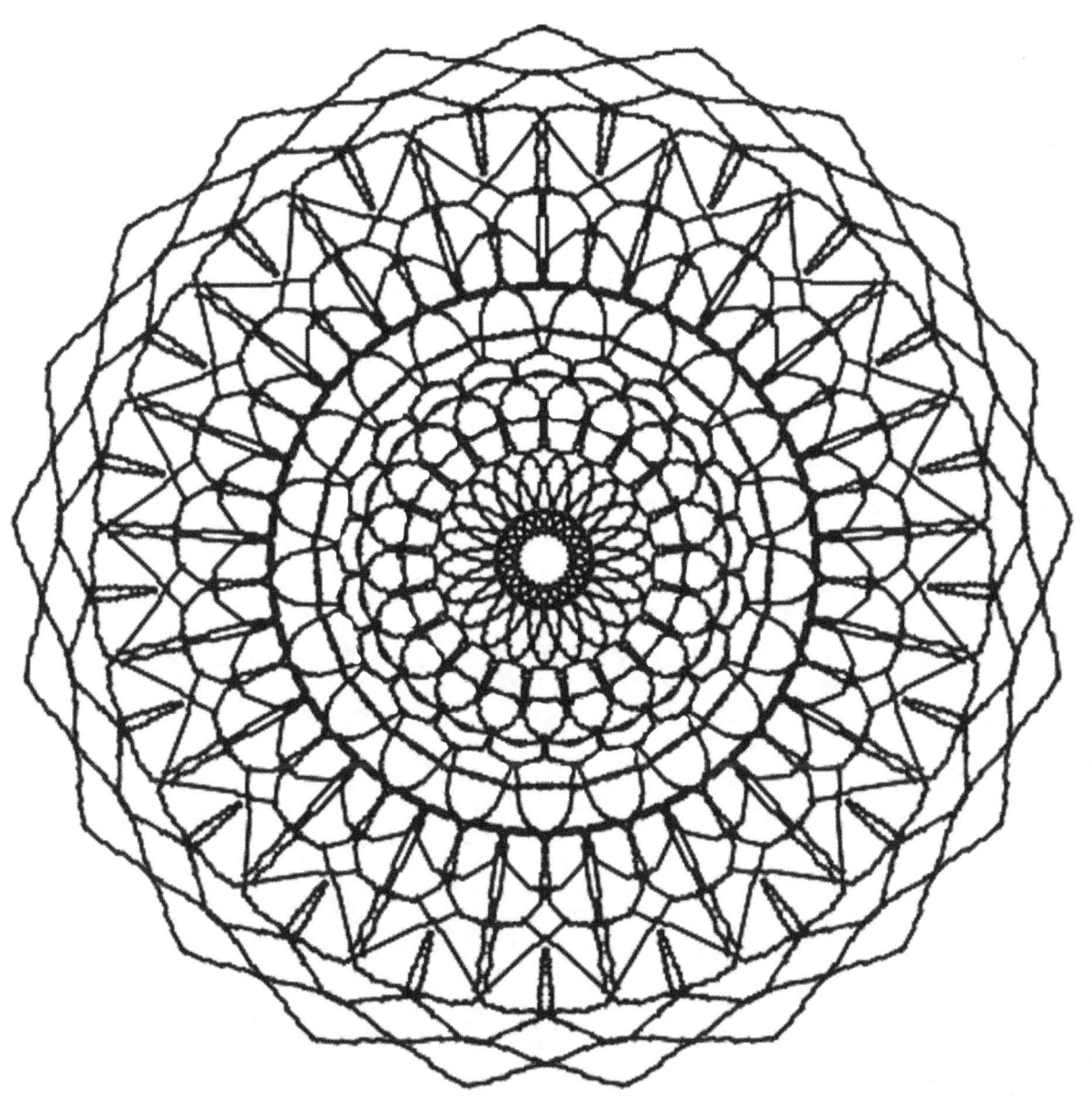

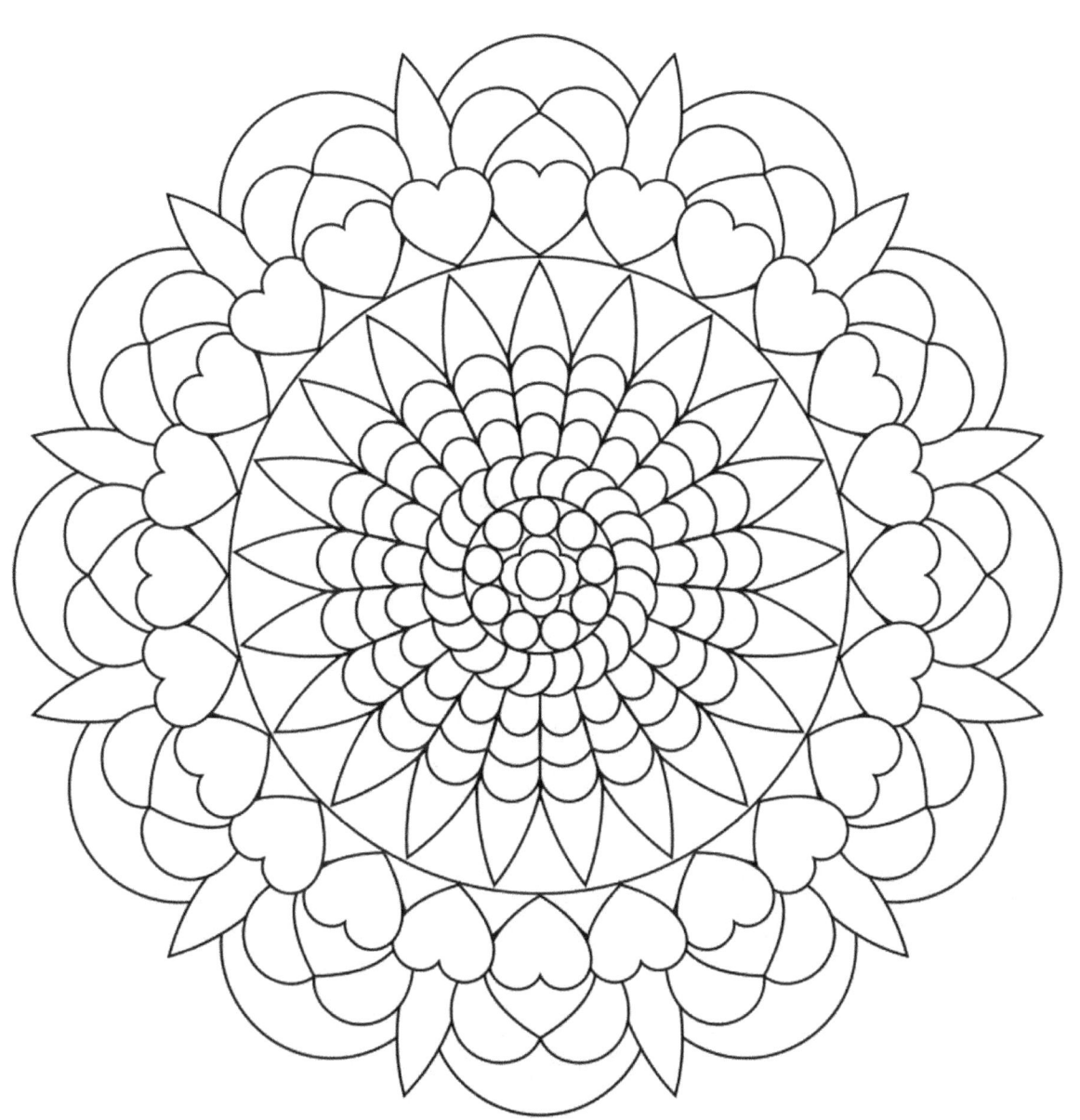

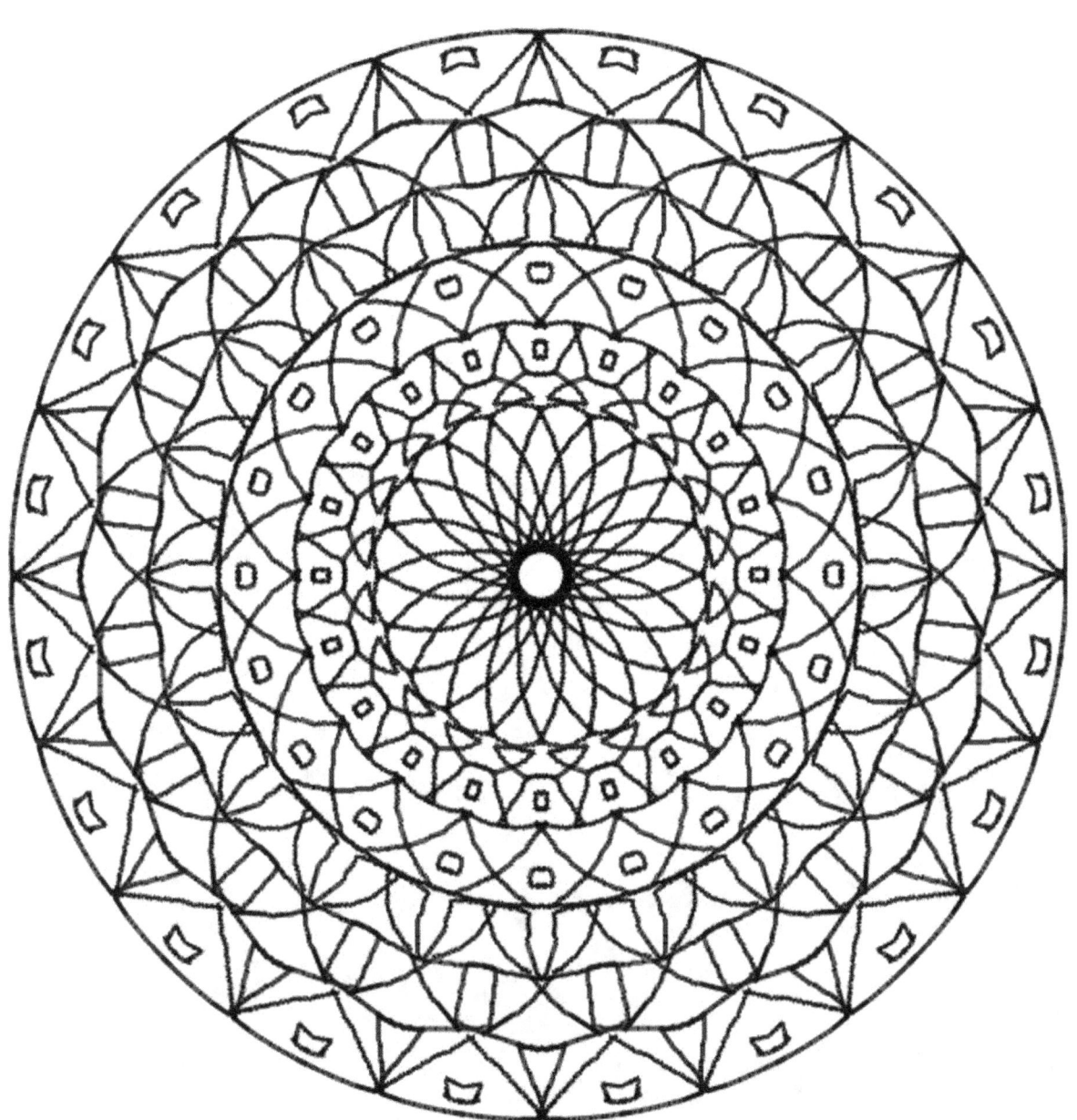

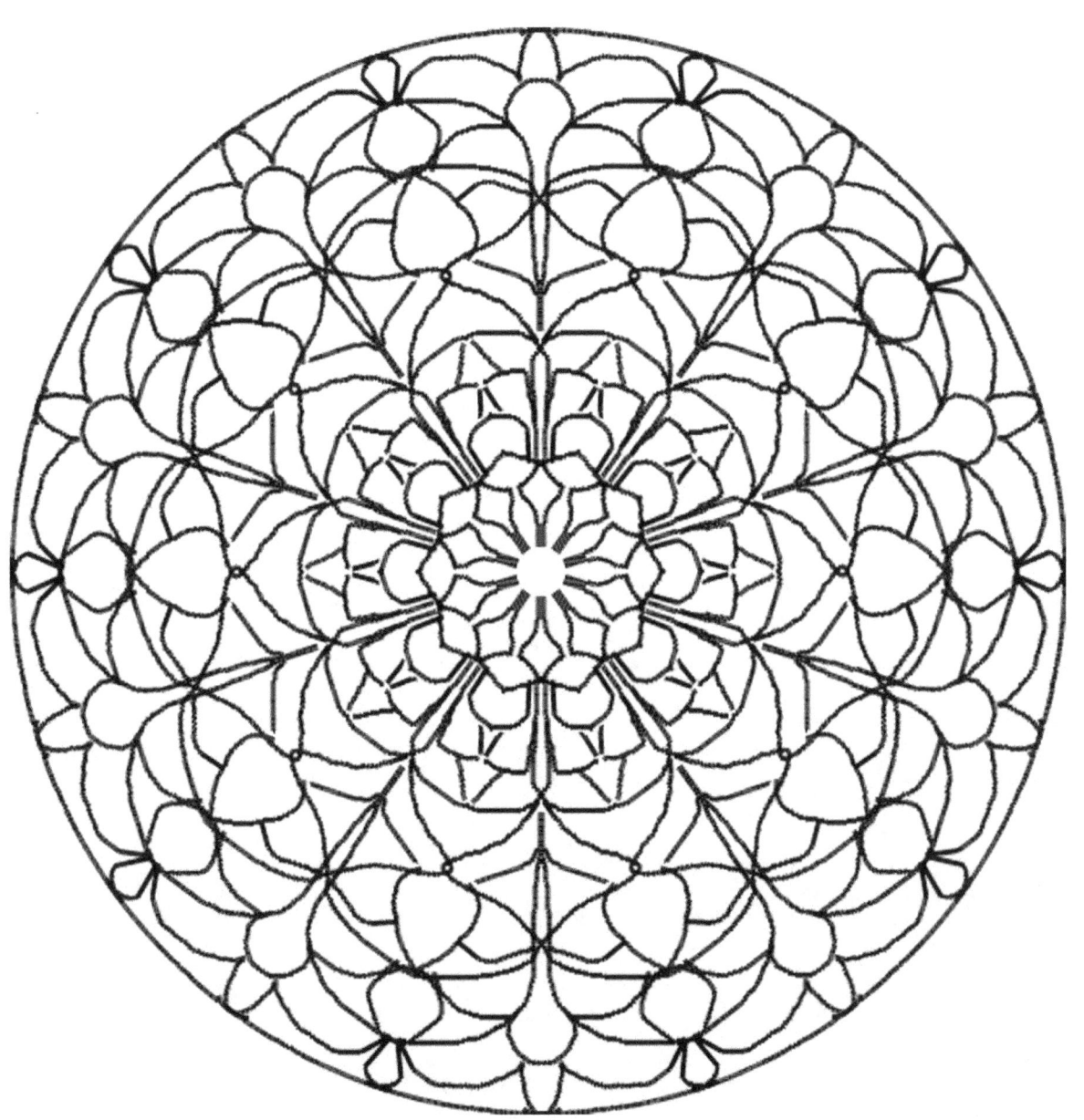

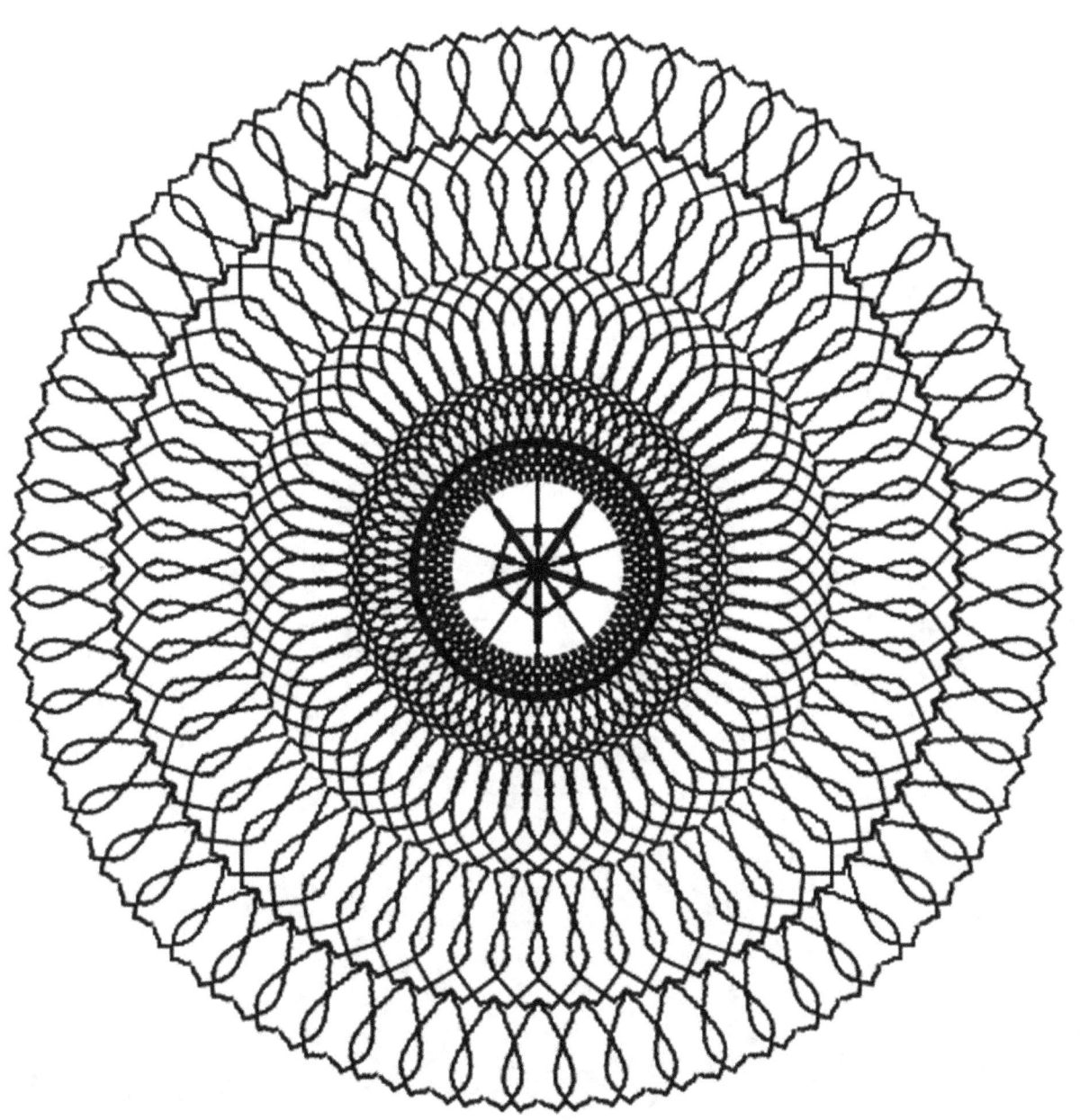

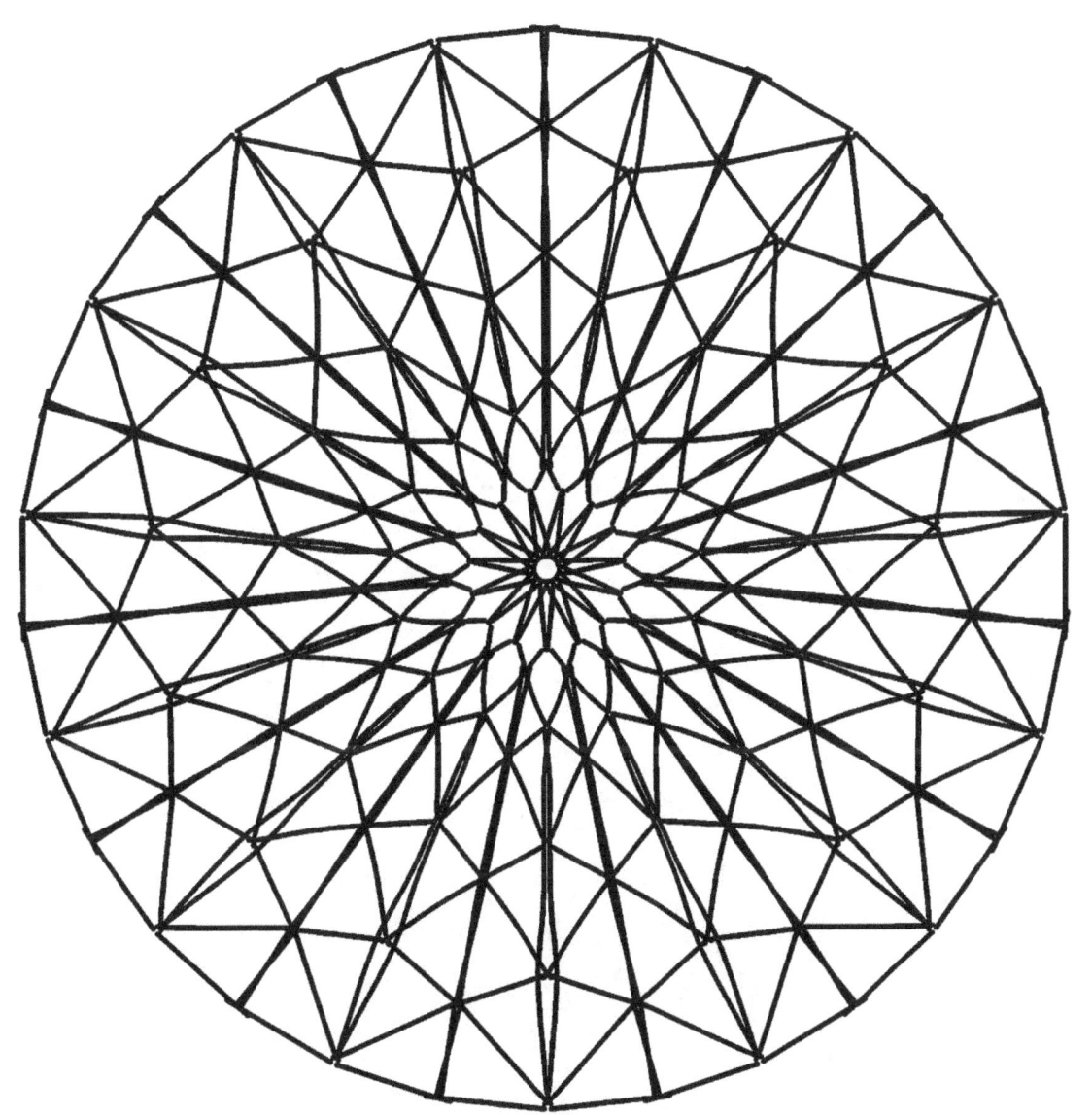

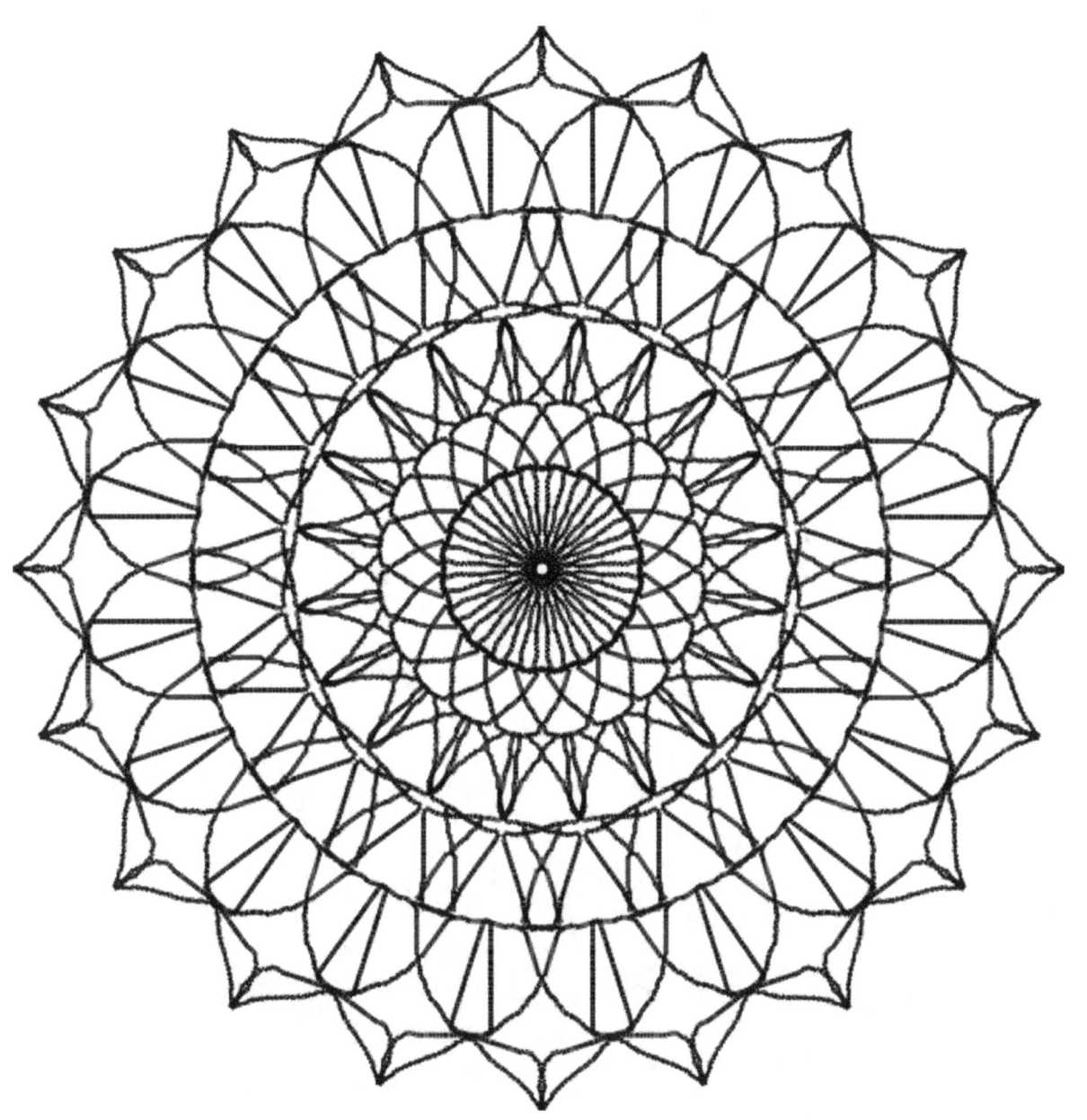

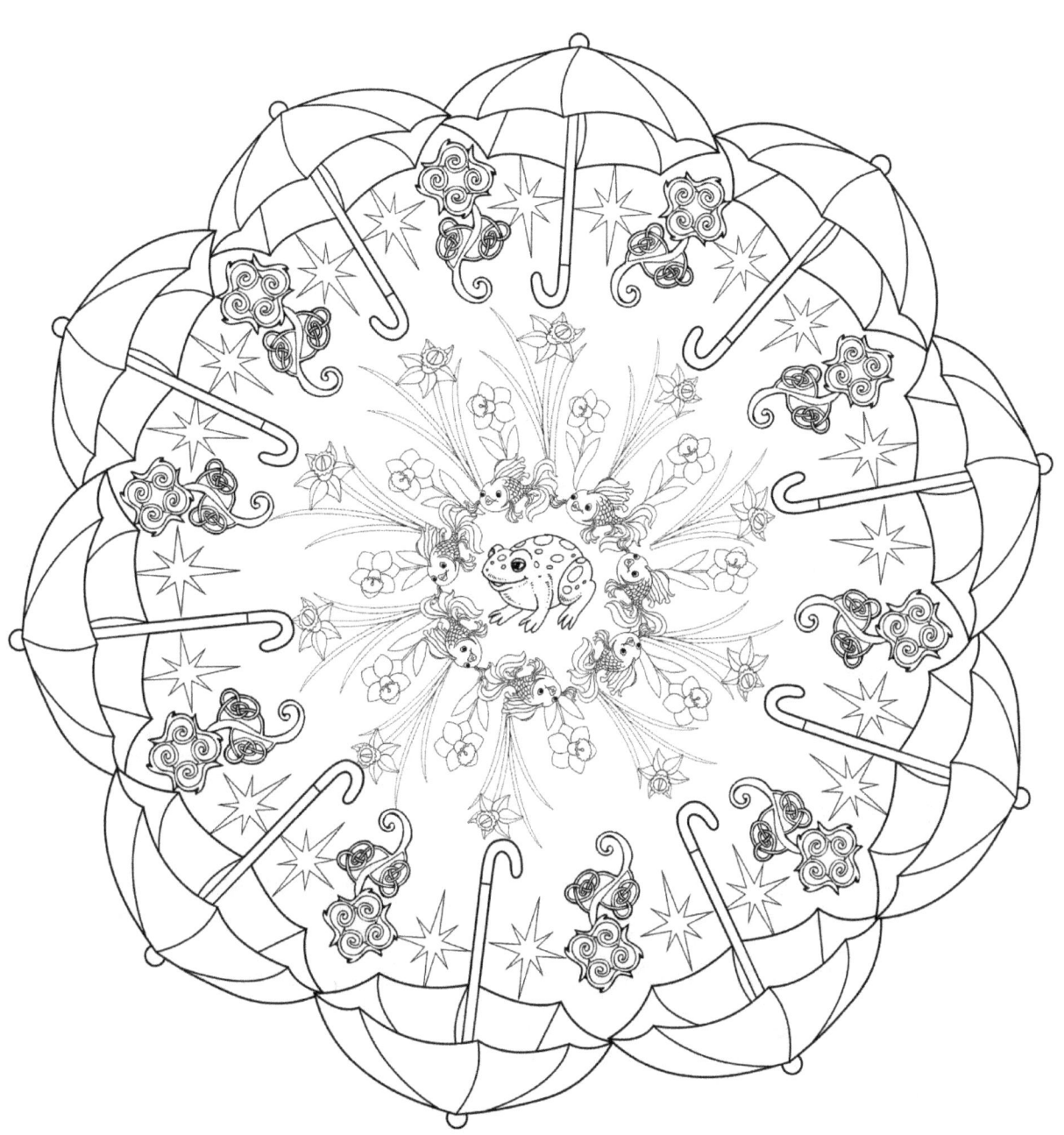

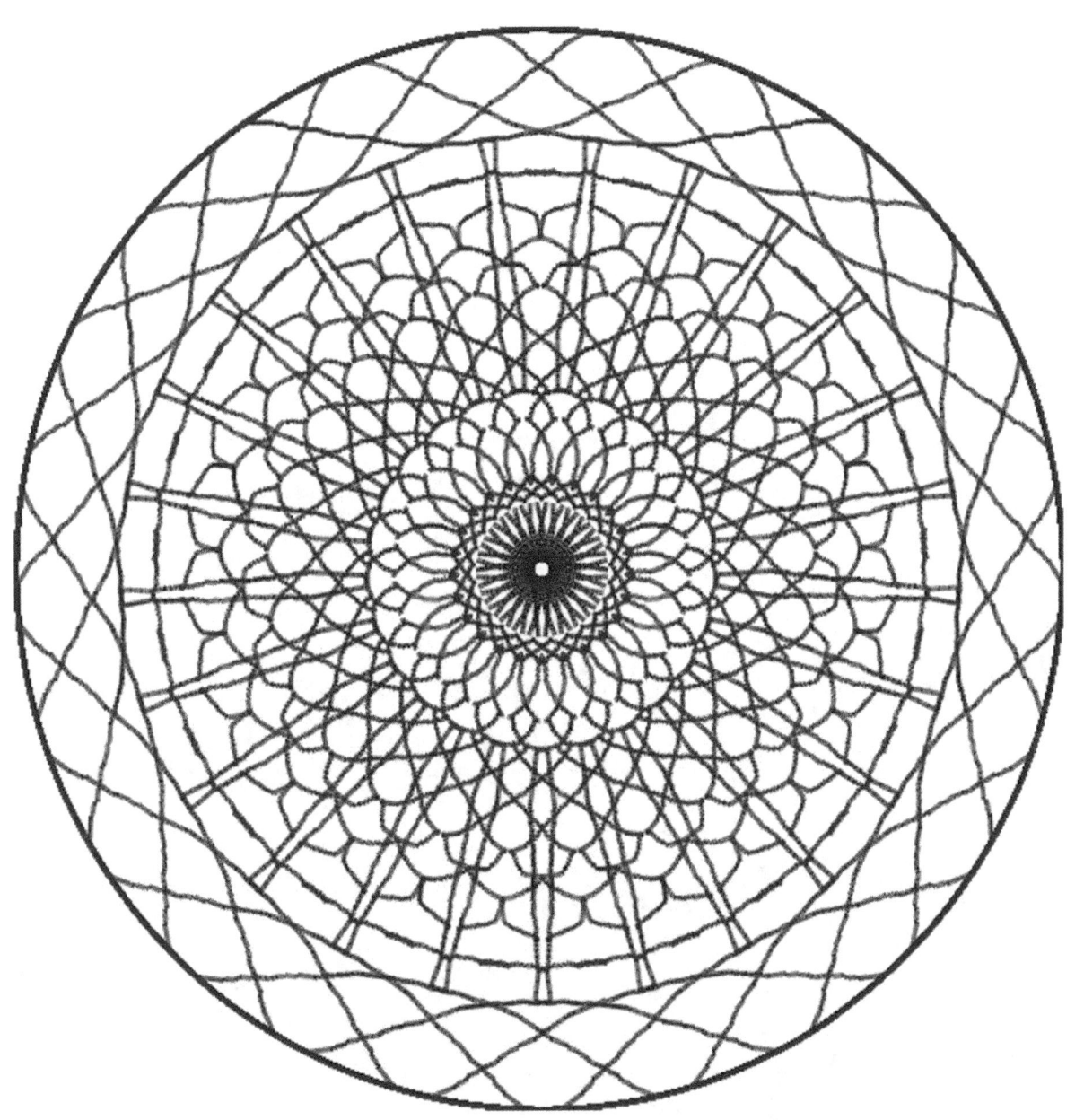

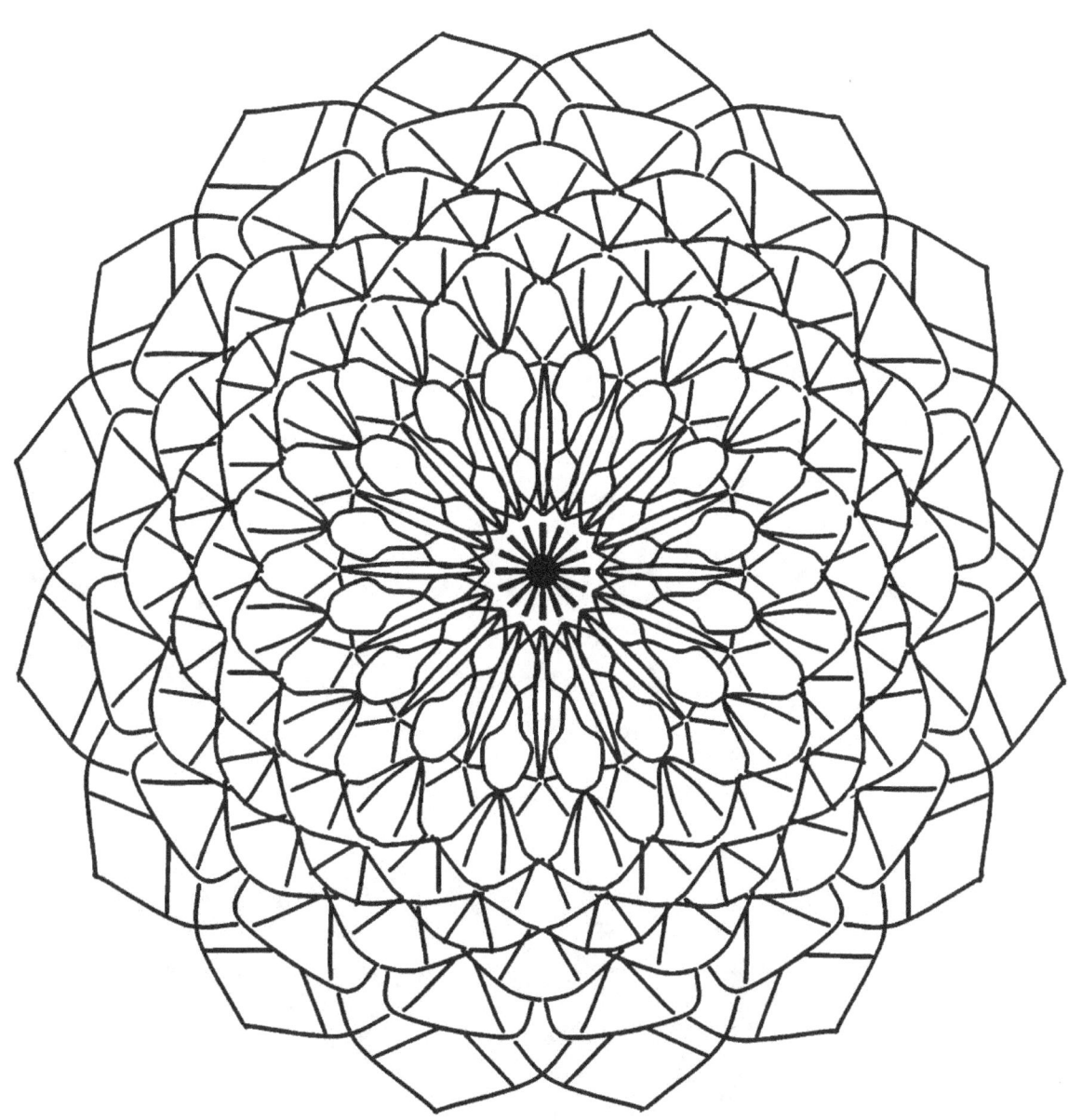

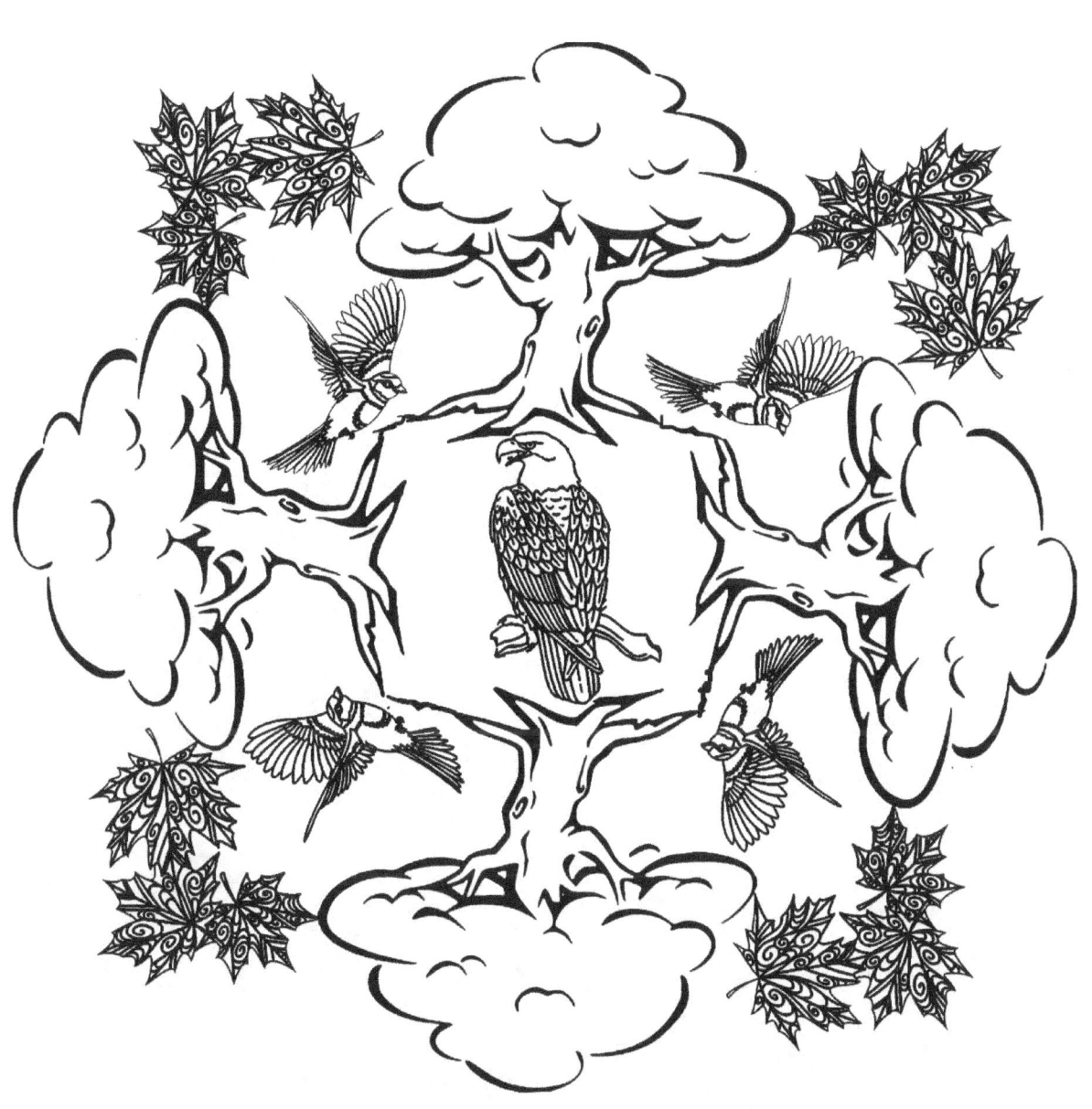

www.ingramcontent.com/pod-product-compliance
Lightning Source LLC
Chambersburg PA
CBHW081255180526
45170CB00007B/2434